THE LIFE OF
OUR LORD

THE LIFE OF
OUR LORD

WRITTEN EXPRESSLY
FOR HIS CHILDREN BY
CHARLES DICKENS

With Foreword and Appendix
by Dr. D. James Kennedy

THE WESTMINSTER PRESS
PHILADELPHIA

First Published in MCMXXXIV by
Associated Newspapers Ltd., London

Foreword and Appendix © 1986 D. James Kennedy

Reproduction of the portrait of Dickens' four eldest
children, by Maclise, has been furnished by
The Dickens House, London, and is used with permission.

Engravings are reproduced from a volume of *The Fireside
Sunday School and Weekly Bible Readings* supplied through
the courtesy of the National Publishing Company, which
began publishing Bibles in Philadelphia during the
lifetime of Charles Dickens.

Published by The Westminster Press®
Philadelphia, Pennsylvania

PRINTED IN THE UNITED STATES OF AMERICA
2 4 6 8 9 7 5 3 1

Library of Congress Catalog Card No. 86-51416
ISBN 0-664-24071-2 (paper)
ISBN 0-664-21727-3 (leather)

2329 Jesus Christ - Biography

FOREWORD

by

Dr. D. JAMES KENNEDY

THE LIFE OF OUR LORD, by Charles Dickens, reflects the personal faith of this great English novelist and his desire to transmit this faith to his children. Dickens' novels show a Christian concern for the poor, an appreciation of the dark effect sin has had on the world, and a demand both for the regeneration of men and for social reform. These themes so fill Dickens' popular works that the Russian author Dostoyevski referred to him as "the Great Christian."

However, until the publication of this work in 1934, eighty-five years after Dickens wrote it, it would have been difficult, if not impossible, to say where he stood on matters of religion. When we read this retelling of the life of Christ, we can better appreciate the section of Dickens' last will and testament in which he commended his soul to God and to the mercy of the Lord Jesus Christ.

Readers should view this book as a paraphrase of the life of Christ done by a father for his children, and not as a doctrinal essay. Dickens was a great novelist, but he never claimed to be an accomplished theologian. As I read this delightful and important book, it seems to me that Dickens, like many people in the church today, was somewhat unclear on the

5

proper relationship between faith and good works. Rather than stating that we are accepted by God through faith alone because of Jesus Christ's payment for our sins on the cross, Dickens sometimes implied that people are saved by their good works. However, in other statements, he did seem to understand that our hope of salvation rests on God's mercy alone. Because these apparent discrepancies could prove confusing, I have included a special appendix to clarify some of the doctrinal points.

With its charming language and simple explanations, *The Life of Our Lord* is a wonderful book to read to our children to help them understand more about Christ. It also encourages us, as parents, to strive to communicate God's truth to our children, even as Dickens did. Finally, as Christians we can rejoice that God allowed Charles Dickens, a writer who had a major impact on Western culture, to feel such a commitment to the ideals of Christ.

FOREWORD

by

LADY DICKENS

THIS book, the last work of Charles Dickens to be published, has an individual interest and purpose that separate it completely from everything else that Dickens wrote.

Quite apart from its Divine Subject, the manuscript is peculiarly personal to the novelist, and is not so much a revelation of his mind as a tribute to his heart and humanity, and also, of course, his deep devotion to Our Lord.

It was written in 1849, twenty-one years before his death, expressly for his children.

The simple manuscript is entirely hand-written, and is in no sense a fair copy but a spontaneous draft. In order to preserve its personality, the manuscript has been followed faithfully in every detail. This accounts for the varying use of capital letters, and other peculiarities.

Charles Dickens frequently told his children the Gospel Story, and made mention of the Divine Example in his letters to them.

This life of Our Lord was written without

thought of publication, in order that his family might have a permanent record of their father's thoughts.

After his death, this manuscript remained in the possession of his sister-in-law, Miss Georgina Hogarth.

On her death in 1917 it came into the possession of Sir Henry Fielding Dickens.

Charles Dickens had made it clear that he had written *The Life of Our Lord* in a form which he thought best suited to his children, and not for publication. His son, Sir Henry, was averse to publishing the work in his own lifetime, but saw no reason why publication should be withheld after his death.

Sir Henry's will provided that, if the majority of his family were in favour of publication, *The Life of Our Lord* should be given to the world. It was first published, in serial form, in March 1934.

Marie Dickens

April 1934.

LIST OF ILLUSTRATIONS

Written for his own Children
by
Charles Dickens
1849

*This inscription appears on the medallion of the case which
contains the manuscript of Charles Dickens'
" Life of Our Lord."*

CHAPTER THE FIRST

Y DEAR CHILDREN, I am very anxious that you should know something about the History of Jesus Christ. For everybody ought to know about Him. No one ever lived, who was so good, so kind, so gentle, and so sorry for all people who did wrong, or were in anyway ill or miserable, as he was. And as he is now in Heaven, where we hope to go, and all to meet each other after we are dead, and there be happy always together, you never can think what a good place Heaven is, without

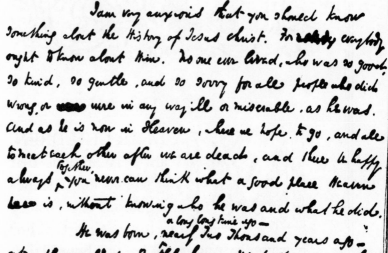

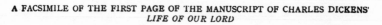

A FACSIMILE OF THE FIRST PAGE OF THE MANUSCRIPT OF CHARLES DICKENS'
LIFE OF OUR LORD

knowing who he was and what he
did.

HE was born, a long long time
ago—nearly Two Thousand years
ago — at a place called Bethlehem.
His father and mother lived in
a city called Nazareth, but they
were forced, by business to travel
to Bethlehem. His father's name
was Joseph, and his mother's name
was Mary. And the town being very
full of people, also brought there by
business, there was no room for Joseph
and Mary in the Inn or in any house ;
so they went into a Stable to lodge,
and in this stable Jesus Christ was
born. There was no cradle or any-
thing of that kind there, so Mary laid
her pretty little boy in what is called
the Manger, which is the place the

horses eat out of. And there he fell
asleep.

While he was asleep, some Shepherds
who were watching Sheep in the Fields,
saw an Angel from God, all light and
beautiful, come moving over the grass
towards Them. At first they were
afraid and fell down and hid their
faces. But it said "There is a child
born to-day in the City of Bethlehem
near here, who will grow up to be
so good that God will love him as
his own son; and he will teach men
to love one another, and not to quarrel
and hurt one another; and his name
will be Jesus Christ; and people will
put that name in their prayers, because
they will know God loves it, and will
know that they should love it too."
And then the Angel told the Shepherds
to go to that Stable, and look at that

14

little child in the Manger. Which they did ; and they kneeled down by it in its sleep, and said " God bless this child ! "

Now the great place of all that country was Jerusalem—just as London is the great place in England—and at Jerusalem the King lived, whose name was King Herod. Some wise men came one day, from a country a long way off in the East, and said to the King " We have seen a Star in the Sky, which teaches us to know that a child is born in Bethlehem who will live to be a man whom all people will love." When King Herod heard this, he was jealous, for he was a wicked man. But he pretended not to be, and said to the wise men, " Whereabouts is this child ? " And the wise men said " We don't know.

But we think the Star will shew us ;
for the Star has been moving on before
us, all the way here, and is now standing still in the sky." Then Herod
asked them to see if the Star would
shew them where the child lived, and
ordered them, if they found the child,
to come back to him. So they went
out, and the Star went on, over their
heads a little way before them, until
it stopped over the house where the
child was. This was very wonderful,
but God ordered it to be so.

When the Star stopped, the wise
men went in, and saw the child with
Mary his Mother. They loved him
very much, and gave him some presents.
Then they went away. But they did
not go back to King Herod ; for they
thought he was jealous, though he had
not said so. So they went away, by

night, back into their own country.
And an Angel came, and told Joseph
and Mary to take the child into a
Country called Egypt, or Herod would
kill him. So they escaped too, in
the night—the father, the mother, and
the child—and arrived there, safely.

But when this cruel Herod found
that the wise men did not come back
to him, and that he could not, therefore, find out where this child, Jesus
Christ, lived, he called his soldiers
and captains to him, and told them
to go and Kill all the children in
his dominions that were not more than
two years old. The wicked men did
so. The mothers of the children ran
up and down the streets with them
in their arms trying to save them,
and hide them in caves and cellars,
but it was of no use. The soldiers

with their swords killed all the children they could find. This dreadful murder was called the Murder of the Innocents. Because the little children were so innocent.

King Herod hoped that Jesus Christ was one of them. But He was not, as you know, for He had escaped safely into Egypt. And he lived there, with his father and mother, until Bad King Herod died.

CHAPTER THE SECOND

WHEN King Herod was dead, an angel came to Joseph again, and said he might now go to Jerusalem, and not be afraid for the child's sake. So Joseph and Mary, and her Son Jesus Christ (who are commonly called The Holy Family) travelled towards Jerusalem; but hearing on the way that King Herod's son was the new King, and fearing that he, too, might want to hurt the child, they turned out of the way, and went to live in Nazareth. They lived there, until Jesus Christ was twelve years old.

THEN Joseph and Mary went to Jerusalem to attend a Religious Feast which used to be held in those days, in the Temple of Jerusalem, which was a great church or Cathedral; and they took Jesus Christ with them. And when the Feast was over, they travelled away from Jerusalem, back towards their own home in Nazareth, with a great many of their friends and neighbours. For people used, then, to travel a great many together, for fear of robbers; the roads not being so safe and well guarded as they are now, and travelling being much more difficult altogether, than it now is.

They travelled on, for a whole day, and never knew that Jesus Christ was not with them; for the company being so large, they thought he was somewhere among the people, though they

20

did not see Him. But finding that he was not there, and fearing that he was lost, they turned back to Jerusalem in great anxiety to look for him. They found him, sitting in the Temple, talking about the goodness of God, and how we should all pray to him, with some learned men who were called Doctors. They were not what you understand by the word " doctors " now ; they did not attend sick people ; they were scholars and clever men. And Jesus Christ shewed such knowledge in what he said to them, and in the questions he asked them, that they were all astonished.

He went, with Joseph and Mary, home to Nazareth, when they had found him, and lived there until he was thirty or thirty-five years old.

AT that time there was a very good man indeed, named John, who was the son of a woman named Elizabeth—the cousin of Mary. And people being wicked, and violent, and killing each other, and not minding their duty towards God, John (to teach them better) went about the country, preaching to them, and entreating them to be better men and women. And because he loved them more than himself, and didn't mind himself when he was doing them good, he was poorly dressed in the skin of a camel, and ate little but some insects called locusts, which he found as he travelled : and wild honey, which the bees left in the Hollow Trees. You never saw a locust, because they belong to that country near Jerusalem, which is a great way off. So do camels, but I think you have seen a camel? At all events they are brought over here, sometimes; and if you would like to see one, I will shew you one.

THERE was a River, not very far from Jerusalem, called the River Jordan; and in this water, John baptized those people who would come to him, and promise to be better. A great many people went to him in crowds. Jesus Christ went too. But when John saw him, John said, " Why should I baptize you, who are so much better than I ! " Jesus Christ made answer, " Suffer it to be so now." So John baptized him. And when he was baptized, the sky opened, and a beautiful bird like a dove came flying down, and the voice of God, speaking up in Heaven, was heard to say " This

23

is my beloved Son, in whom I am well pleased!"

Jesus Christ then went into a wild and lonely country called the Wilderness, and stayed there forty days and forty nights, praying that he might be of use to men and women, and teach them to be better, so that after their deaths, they might be happy in Heaven.

WHEN he came out of the Wilderness, he began to cure sick people by only laying his hand upon them; for God had given him power to heal the sick, and to give sight to the blind, and to do many wonderful and solemn things of which I shall tell you more bye and bye, and which are called "*The Miracles*" of Christ. I wish you would remember that word, be-

24

cause I shall use it again, and I should like you to know that it means something which is very wonderful and which could not be done without God's leave and assistance.

The first miracle which Jesus Christ did, was at a place called Cana, where he went to a Marriage-Feast with Mary his Mother. There was no wine; and Mary told him so. There were only six stone water-pots filled with water. But Jesus turned this water into wine, by only lifting up his hand; and all who were there, drank of it.

For God had given Jesus Christ the power to do such wonders; and he did them, that people might know he was not a common man, and might believe what he taught them, and also believe that God had sent him. And

25

many people, hearing this, and hearing that he cured the sick, did begin to believe in him ; and great crowds followed him in the streets and on the roads, wherever he went.

CHAPTER THE THIRD

THAT there might be some good men to go about with Him, teaching the people, Jesus Christ chose Twelve poor men to be his companions. These twelve are called *The apostles* or *Disciples*, and he chose them from among Poor Men, in order that the Poor might know —always after that; in all years to come—that Heaven was made for them as well as for the rich, and that God makes no difference between those who wear good clothes and those who go barefoot and in rags. The most miser-

able, the most ugly, deformed, wretched
creatures that live, will be bright Angels
in Heaven if they are good here on
earth. Never forget this, when you
are grown up. Never be proud or
unkind, my dears, to any poor man,
woman, or child. If they are bad,
think that they would have been better,
if they had had kind friends, and good
homes, and had been better taught.
So, always try to make them better
by kind persuading words ; and always
try to teach them and relieve them if
you can. And when people speak ill of
the Poor and Miserable, think how Jesus
Christ went among them and taught
them, and thought them worthy of his
care. And always pity them yourselves,
and think as well of them as you can.

The names of the Twelve apostles
were, Simon Peter, Andrew, James the

son of Zebedee, John, Philip, Bartholomew, Thomas, Mathew, James the son of Alphaeus, Labbæus, Simon, and Judas Iscariot. This man afterwards betrayed Jesus Christ, as you will hear bye and bye.

THE first four of these, were poor fishermen, who were sitting in their boats by the seaside, mending their nets, when Christ passed by. He stopped, and went into Simon Peter's boat, and asked him if he had caught many fish. Peter said No ; though they had worked all night with their nets, they had caught nothing. Christ said, " let down the net again." They did so ; and it was immediately so full of fish, that it required the strength of many men (who came and helped them) to lift it out of the water, and even

29

then it was very hard to do. This was another of the miracles of Jesus Christ.

Jesus then said " Come with me." And they followed him directly. And from that time the Twelve disciples or apostles were always with him.

AS great crowds of people followed him, and wished to be taught, he went up into a Mountain and there preached to them, and gave them, from his own lips, the words of that Prayer, beginning " Our father which art in Heaven," that you say every night. It is called The Lord's Prayer, because it was first said by Jesus Christ, and because he commanded his disciples to pray in those words.

When he was come down from the Mountain, there came to him a man with a dreadful disease called the

30

leprosy. It was common in those times, and those who were ill with it, were called lepers. This Leper fell at the feet of Jesus Christ, and said " Lord ! If thou wilt, thou cans't make me well ! " Jesus, always full of compassion, stretched out his hand, and said " I will ! Be thou well ! " And his disease went away, immediately, and he was cured.

BEING followed, wherever he went, by great crowds of people, Jesus went, with his disciples, into a house, to rest. While he was sitting inside, some men brought upon a bed, a man who was very ill of what is called the Palsy, so that he trembled all over from head to foot, and could neither stand, nor move. But the crowd being all about the door and windows, and they not being able to get near Jesus Christ, these men climbed up to the roof of the house, which was a low one ; and through the tiling at the top, let down the bed, with the sick man upon it, into the room where Jesus sat. When he saw him, Jesus, full of pity, said " Arise ! Take up thy bed, and go to thine own home ! " And the man rose up and went away quite well ; blessing him, and thanking God.

THERE was a Centurion too, or officer over the Soldiers, who came to him, and said, " Lord ! My servant lies at home in my house, very ill."—Jesus Christ made answer, " I will come and cure him." But the Centurion said " Lord ! I am not worthy that Thou shoulds't come to my house. Say the word only, and I know he will be cured." Then Jesus Christ, glad that the Centurion believed in him so truly, said " Be it so ! " And the servant became well, from that moment.

But of all the people who came to him, none were so full of grief and distress, as one man who was a Ruler or Magistrate over many people, and he wrung his hands, and cried, and said " Oh Lord, my daughter—my beautiful, good, innocent little girl, is .dead. Oh come to her, come to her, and lay Thy blessed hand upon her, and I know she will revive, and come to life again, and make me and her mother happy. Oh Lord we love her so, we love her so ! And she is dead ! "

Jesus Christ went out with him, and so did his disciples and went to his house, where the friends and neighbours were crying in the room where

33

the poor dead little girl lay, and where there was soft music playing ; as there used to be, in those days, when people died. Jesus Christ, looking on her, sorrowfully, said—to comfort her poor parents—" She is not dead. She is asleep." Then he commanded the room to be cleared of the people that were in it, and going to the dead child, took her by the hand, and she rose up, quite well, as if she had only been asleep. Oh what a sight it must have been to see her parents clasp her in their arms, and kiss her, and thank God, and Jesus Christ his son, for such great Mercy !

But he was always merciful and tender. And because he did such Good, and taught people how to love God and how to hope to go to Heaven after death, he was called *Our Saviour*.

CHAPTER THE FOURTH

THERE were in that, country where Our Saviour performed his Miracles, certain people who were called Pharisees. They were very proud, and believed that no people were good but themselves; and they were all afraid of Jesus Christ, because he taught the people better. So were the Jews, in general. Most of the Inhabitants of that country, were Jews.

Our Saviour, walking once in the fields with his disciples on a Sunday (which the Jews called, and still call, the Sabbath) they gathered some ears of the corn that was growing there, to eat. This, the Pharisees said, was wrong; and in the same way, when our Saviour went into one of their churches—they were called Synagogues —and looked compassionately on a poor man who had his hand all withered and wasted away, these Pharisees said " Is it right to cure people on a Sunday ? " Our Saviour answered them by saying, " If any of you had a sheep and it fell into a pit, would you not take it out, even though it happened on a Sunday ? And how much better is a man than a sheep ! " Then he said to the poor man, " Stretch out thine hand ! " And it was cured immediately, and was smooth and useful like the other. So Jesus Christ told them " You may always do good, no matter what the day is."

THERE was a city called Nain into which Our Saviour went soon after this, followed by great numbers of people, and especially by those who had sick relations, or friends, or children. For they brought sick people out into the streets and roads through which he passed, and cried out to him to touch them, and when he did, they became well. Going on, in the midst of this crowd, and near the Gate of the city, He met a funeral. It was the funeral of a young man, who was carried on what is called a Bier, which was open, as the custom was in that country, and is now in many parts of Italy. His poor mother followed the bier, and wept very much, for she had no other child. When Our Saviour saw her, he was touched to the heart to see her so sorry, and

said " Weep not ! " Then, the bearers
of the bier standing still, he walked
up to it and touched it with his hand,
and said " Young Man ! Arise." The
dead man, coming to life again at
the sound of The Saviour's Voice,
rose up and began to speak. And
Jesus Christ leaving him with his
mother—Ah how happy they both
were !—went away.

By this time the crowd was so very
great that Jesus Christ went down to
the waterside, to go in a boat, to
a more retired place. And in the
boat, He fell asleep, while his Disciples
were sitting on the deck. While he
was still sleeping a violent storm arose,
so that the waves washed over the
boat, and the howling wind so rocked
and shook it, that they thought it
would sink. In their fright the dis-

38

ciples awoke Our Saviour, and said
" Lord ! Save us, or we are lost ! "
He stood up, and raising his arm,
said to the rolling Sea and to the
whistling wind, " Peace ! Be still ! "
And immediately it was calm and pleasant weather, and the boat went safely
on, through the smooth waters.

When they came to the other side
of the waters they had to pass a wild
and lonely burying-ground that was
outside the City to which they were
going. All burying-grounds were outside cities in those times. In this
place there was a dreadful madman
who lived among the tombs, and houled
all day and night, so that it made
travellers afraid, to hear him. They
had tried to chain him, but he broke
his chains, he was so strong ; and
he would throw himself on the sharp

stones, and cut himself in the most dreadful manner : crying and houling all the while : When this wretched man saw Jesus Christ a long way off, he cried out " It is the son of God ! Oh son of God, do not torment me ! " Jesus, coming near him, perceived that he was torn by an Evil Spirit, and cast the madness out of him, and into a herd of swine (or pigs) who were feeding close by, and who directly ran headlong down a steep place leading to the sea and were dashed to pieces.

NOW Herod, the son of that cruel King who murdered the Innocents, reigning over the people there, and hearing that Jesus Christ was doing these wonders, and was giving sight to the blind and causing the deaf to hear, and the dumb to speak, and

the lame to walk, and that he was
followed by multitudes and multitudes
of people—Herod, hearing this, said
" This man is a companion and friend
of John the Baptist." John was the
good man, you recollect, who wore
a garment made of camel's hair, and
ate wild honey. Herod had taken him
Prisoner, because he taught and preached
to the people ; and had him then,
locked up, in the prisons of his Palace.

WHILE Herod was in this angry
humour with John, his birthday
came ; and his daughter, Herodias, who
was a fine dancer, danced before him, to
please him. She pleased him so much
that he swore an oath he would give
her whatever she would ask him for.
" Then ", said she, " father, give me
the head of John the Baptist in a

charger." For she hated John, and was a wicked, cruel woman.

The King was sorry, for though he had John prisoner, he did not wish to kill him ; but having sworn that he would give her what she asked for, he sent some soldiers down into the Prison, with directions to cut off the head of John the Baptist, and give it to Herodias. This they did, and took it to her, as she had said, in a charger, which was a kind of dish. When Jesus Christ heard from the apostles of this cruel deed, he left that city, and went with them (after they had privately buried John's body in the night) to another place.

CHAPTER THE FIFTH

ONE of the Pharisees begged Our Saviour to go into his house, and eat with him. And while our Saviour sat eating at the table, there crept into the room a woman of that city who had led a bad and sinful life, and was ashamed that the Son of God should see her; and yet she trusted so much to his goodness, and his compassion for all who, having done wrong were truly sorry for it in their hearts, that, by little and little, she went behind the seat on which he sat, and dropped

43

down at his feet, and wetted them with her sorrowful tears ; then she kissed them and dried them on her long hair, and rubbed them with some sweet-smelling ointment she had brought with her in a box. Her name was Mary Magdalene.

When the Pharisee saw that Jesus permitted this woman to touch Him, he said within himself that Jesus did not know how wicked she had been. But Jesus Christ, who knew his thoughts, said to him " Simon "—for that was his name—" if a man had debtors, one of whom owed him five hundred pence, and one of whom owed him only fifty pence, and he forgave them, both, their debts, which of those two debtors do you think would love him most ? " Simon answered " I suppose that one whom he forgave most." Jesus told him he was right, and said " As God forgives this woman so much sin, she will love Him, I hope, the more." And he said to her, " God forgives you ! " The company who were present wondered that Jesus Christ had power to forgive sins, but God had given it to Him. And the woman thanking Him for all his mercy, went away.

WE learn from this, that we must always forgive those who have done us any harm, when they come to us and say they are truly sorry for it. Even if they do not come and say so, we must still forgive them, and never hate them or be unkind to them, if we would hope that God will forgive us.

After this there was a great feast

of the Jews, and Jesus Christ went
to Jerusalem. There was, near the
sheep market in that place, a pool,
or pond, called Bethesda, having five
gates to it; and at the time of the
year when that feast took place great
numbers of sick people and cripples
went to this pool to bathe in it:
believing that an Angel came and
stirred the water, and that whoever
went in first after the Angel had done
so, was cured of any illness he or she
had, whatever it might be. Among
these poor persons, was one man who
had been ill, thirty eight years; and
he told Jesus Christ (who took pity
on him when he saw him lying on
his bed alone, with no one to help
him) that he never could be dipped
in the pool, because he was so weak
and ill that he could not move to

46

get there. Our Saviour said to him,
" take up thy bed and go away." And
he went away, quite well.

MANY Jews saw this ; and when
they saw it, they hated Jesus Christ
the more : knowing that the people,
being taught and cured by him, would
not believe their Priests, who told the
people what was not true, and deceived
them. So they said to one another
that Jesus Christ should be killed, because he cured people on the Sabbath
Day (which was against their strict
law) and because he called himself
the Son of God. And they tried to
raise enemies against him, and to get
the crowd in the streets to murder
Him.

But the crowd followed Him where-
ever he went, blessing him, and praying

47

to be taught and cured ; for they knew He did nothing but Good. Jesus going with his disciples over a sea, called the Sea of Tiberias and sitting with them on a hill-side, saw great numbers of these poor people waiting below, and said to the apostle Philip, " Where shall we buy bread, that they may eat and be refreshed, after their long journey ? " Philip answered, " Lord, two hundred pennyworth of bread would not be enough for so many people, and we have none." " We have only ", said another apostle —Andrew, Simon Peter's brother— " five small barley loaves, and two little fish, belonging to a lad who is among us. What are they, among so many ! " Jesus Christ said, " Let them all sit down ! " They did ; there being a great deal of grass in that place.

When they were all seated, Jesus took the bread, and looked up to Heaven, and blessed it, and broke it, and handed it in pieces to the apostles, who handed it to the people. And of those five little loaves, and two fish, five thousand men, besides women, and children, ate, and had enough ; and when they were all satisfied, there were gathered up twelve baskets full of what was left. This was another of the Miracles of Jesus Christ.

OUR Saviour then sent his disciples away in a boat, across the water, and said he would follow them presently, when he had dismissed the people. The people being gone, he remained by himself to pray ; so that the night came on, and the disciples were still rowing on the water in their boat, wondering when Christ would come. Late in the night, when the wind was against them and the waves were running high, they saw Him coming walking towards them on the water, as if it were dry land. When they saw this, they were terrified, and cried out, but Jesus said, " It is I. Be not afraid ! " Peter taking courage, said, " Lord, if it be thou, tell me to come to thee upon the water." Jesus Christ said, " Come ! " Peter then walked towards Him, but seeing the angry waves, and hearing the wind roar, he was frightened and began to sink, and would have done so, but that Jesus took him by the hand, and led him into the boat. Then, in a moment, the wind went down ; and the Disciples said to one another, " It is true ! He is the Son of God ! "

JESUS did many more miracles after this happened and cured the sick in great numbers : making the lame walk, and the dumb speak, and the blind see. And being again surrounded by a great crowd who were faint and hungry, and had been with him for three days eating little, he took from his disciples seven loaves and a few fish, and again divided them among the people who were four thousand in number. They all ate, and had enough ; and of what was left, there were gathered up seven baskets full.

He now divided the disciples, and sent them into many towns and villages, teaching the people, and giving them power to cure, in the name of God, all those who were ill. And at this time He began to tell them (for he knew what would happen) that he must

51

one day go back to Jerusalem where he would suffer a great deal, and where he would certainly be put to Death. But he said to them that on the third day after he was dead, he would rise from the grave, and ascend to Heaven, where he would sit at the right hand of God, beseeching God's pardon to sinners.

CHAPTER THE SIXTH

SIX days after the last Miracle of the loaves and fish, Jesus Christ went up into a high Mountain, with only three of the Disciples —Peter, James, and John. And while he was speaking to them there, suddenly His face began to shine as if it were the Sun, and the robes he wore, which were white, glistened and shone like sparkling silver, and he stood before them like an angel. A bright cloud overshadowed them at the same time ; and a voice, speaking from the cloud, was heard to say " This is my beloved Son in whom

53

I am well pleased. Hear ye him!" At which the three disciples fell on their knees and covered their faces : being afraid.

This is called the Transfiguration of our Saviour.

When they were come down from this mountain, and were among the people again, a man knelt at the feet of Jesus Christ, and said, " Lord have mercy on my son, for he is mad and cannot help himself, and sometimes falls into the fire, and sometimes into the water, and covers himself with scars and sores. Some of Thy Disciples have tried to cure him, but could not." Our Saviour cured the child immediately ; and turning to his disciples told them they had not been able to cure him themselves, because they did not believe in Him so truly as he had hoped.

54

THE Disciples asked him, " Master, who is greatest in the Kingdom of Heaven ? " Jesus called a little child to him, and took him in his arms, and stood him among them, and answered, " a child like this. I say unto you that none but those who are as humble as little children shall enter into Heaven. Whosoever shall receive one such little child in my name receiveth me. But whosoever hurts one of them, it were better for him that he had a millstone tied about his neck, and were drowned in the depths of the sea. The angels are all children." Our Saviour loved the child, and loved all children. Yes, and all the world. No one ever loved all people, so well and so truly as He did.

Peter asked Him, " Lord, How often shall I forgive any one who offends

me ? Seven times ? " Our Saviour
answered " Seventy times seven times,
and more than that. For how can
you hope that God will forgive you,
when you do wrong, unless you forgive
all other people ! "

And he told his disciples this Story—
He said, there was once a Servant
who owed his master a great deal of
money, and could not pay it. at which
the Master, being very angry, was going
to have this servant sold for a Slave.
But the servant kneeling down and
begging his Master's pardon with great
sorrow, the Master forgave him. Now
this same servant had a fellow-servant
who owed him a hundred pence, and
instead of being kind and forgiving
to this poor man, as his Master had
been to him, he put him in prison
for the debt. His master hearing of

56

it, went to him, and said " oh wicked Servant, I forgave you. Why did you not forgive your fellow servant ! " And because he had not done so, his Master turned him away with great misery. " So," said Our Saviour ; " how can you expect God to forgive you, if you do not forgive others ! " This is the meaning of that part of the Lord's prayer, where we say " forgive us our trespasses "—that word means faults— " as we forgive them that trespass against us."

AND he told them another story, and said ' There was a certain Farmer once, who had a Vineyard, and he went out early in the morning, and agreed with some labourers to work there all day, for a Penny. And bye and bye, when it was later, he went out again and engaged some more labourers on the same terms ; and bye and bye went out again ; and so on, several times, until the afternoon. When the day was over, and they all came to be paid, those who had worked since morning complained that those who had not begun to work until late in the day had the same money as themselves, and they said it was not fair. But the Master, said, " Friend, I agreed with you for a Penny ; and is it less money to you, because I give the same money to another man ? "

Our Saviour meant to teach them by this, that people who have done good all their lives long, will go to Heaven after they are dead. But that people who have been wicked, because of their being miserable, or not having

58

parents and friends to take care of them when young, and who are truly sorry for it, however late in their lives, and pray God to forgive them, will be forgiven and will go to Heaven too. He taught His disciples in these stories, because he knew the people liked to hear them, and would remember what He said better, if he said it in that way. They are called Parables — THE PARABLES OF OUR SAVIOUR; and I wish you to remember that word, as I shall soon have some more of these Parables to tell you about.

The people listened to all that our Saviour said, but were not agreed among themselves about Him. The Pharisees and Jews had spoken to some of them against Him, and some of them were inclined to do Him harm and even to murder Him. But they were afraid, as yet, to do Him any harm, because of His goodness, and His looking so divine and grand—although he was very simply dressed; almost like the poor people—that they could hardly bear to meet his eyes.

One morning, He was sitting in a place called the Mount of Olives, teaching the people who were all clustered round Him, listening and learning attentively, when a great noise was heard, and a crowd of Pharisees, and some other people like them, called Scribes, came running in, with great cries and shouts, dragging among them a woman who had done wrong, and they all cried out together, " Master ! Look at this woman. The law says she shall be pelted with stones until she is dead. But what say you ? what say you ? "

Jesus looked upon the noisy crowd attentively, and knew that they had come to make Him say the law was wrong and cruel ; and that if He said so, they would make it a charge against Him and would kill him. They were ashamed and afraid as He looked into their faces, but they still cried out, " Come ! What say you Master ? what say you ? "

JESUS stooped down, and wrote with his finger in the sand on the ground, " He that is without sin among you, let him throw the first stone at her." As they read this, looking over one another's shoulders, and as He repeated the words to them, they went away, one by one, ashamed, until not a man of all the noisy crowd was left there ; and Jesus Christ, and the woman, hiding her face in her hands, alone remained.

Then said Jesus Christ, " Woman, where are thine accusers ? Hath no man condemned Thee ? " She answered, trembling, " No, Lord ! " Then said our Saviour, " Neither do *I* condemn Thee. Go ! and sin no more ! "

CHAPTER THE SEVENTH

AS Our Saviour sat teach-
ing the people and answer-
ing their questions, a certain
Lawyer stood up, and said
" Master what shall I do,
that I may live again in happiness after
I am dead ? " Jesus said to him " *The
first of all the commandments is, the Lord
our God is one Lord : and Thou shalt love
the Lord Thy God with all Thy heart,
and with all Thy Soul, and with all thy
mind, and with all thy Strength.   And
the second is like unto it.   Thou shalt love
thy neighbour as thyself.   There is none
other commandment greater than these.*"

63

Then the Lawyer said "But who *is* my neighbour? Tell me that I may know." Jesus answered in this Parable: "There was once a traveller," he said, "journeying from Jerusalem to Jericho, who fell among Thieves; and they robbed him of his clothes, and wounded him, and went away, leaving him half dead upon the road. A Priest, happening to pass that way, while the poor man lay there, saw him, but took no notice, and passed by, on the other side. Another man, a Levite, came that way, and also saw him; but he only looked at him for a moment, and then passed by, also. But a certain Samaritan who came travelling along that road, no sooner saw him than he had compassion on him, and dressed his wounds with oil and wine, and set him on the beast he rode himself,

64

and took him to an Inn, and next morning took out of his pocket Two pence and gave them to the Land-lord, saying 'take care of him and whatever you may spend beyond this, in doing so, I will repay you when I come here again."—Now which of these three men," said our Saviour to the Lawyer, " do you think should be called the neighbour of him who fell among the Thieves ? " The Lawyer said, " The man who shewed com-passion on him." " True," replied our Saviour. " Go Thou and do likewise ! Be compassionate to all men. For all men are your neighbours and brothers."

AND he told them this Parable, of which the meaning is, that we are never to be proud, or think ourselves very good, before God, but are always to be humble. He said, "when you are invited to a Feast or Wedding, do not sit down in the best place, lest some more honored man should come, and claim that seat. But sit down in the lowest place, and a better will be offered you if you deserve it. For whosoever exalteth himself shall be abased, and whosoever humbleth himself shall be exalted."

He also told them this Parable.— "There was a certain man who prepared a great supper, and invited many people, and sent his Servant round to them when supper was ready to tell them they were waited for. Upon this, they made excuses. One said he had bought a piece of ground and must go to look at it. Another that he had bought five yoke of Oxen, and must go to try them. Another,

66

that he was newly married, and could not come. When the Master of the house heard this, he was angry, and told the servant to go into the streets, and into the high roads, and among the hedges, and invite the poor, the lame, the maimed, and the blind to supper instead."

The meaning of Our Saviour in telling them this Parable, was, that those who are too busy with their own profits and pleasures, to think of God and of doing good, will not find such favor with him as the sick and miserable.

It happened that our Saviour, being in the city of Jericho, saw, looking down upon him over the heads of the crowd, from a tree into which he had climbed for that purpose, a man named Zacchæus, who was regarded

67

as a common kind of man, and a Sinner, but to whom Jesus Christ called out, as He passed along, that He would come and eat with him in his house that day. Those proud men, the Pharisees and Scribes, hearing this, muttered among themselves, and said " he eats with Sinners." In answer to them, Jesus related this Parable, which is usually called THE PARABLE OF THE PRODIGAL SON.

" THERE was once a Man ", he told them, " who had two sons : and the younger of them said one day, ' Father, give me my share of your riches now, and let me do with it what I please ? The father granting his request, he travelled away with his money into a distant country, and soon spent it in riotous living.

68

this Parable was, that those who are too busy with their own profits and pleasures, to think of God and of doing good, will not find such favor with him as the sick and miserable.

It happened that our Saviour, being in the city of Jericho, saw, looking down upon him over the heads of the crowd, from a tree into which he had climbed for that purpose, a man named Zacchaeus who was regarded as a common kind of man, and a Sinner, but to whom Jesus Christ called out, as He passed along, that He would come and eat with him in his house that day. Those proud men, the Pharisees and Scribes, hearing this, muttered among themselves, and said "he eats with Sinners". In answer to them, Jesus related this Parable, which is usually called The Parable of the Prodigal Son.

"There was once a man" he told them, "who had two sons; and the younger of them said one day 'Father, give me my share of your riches now, and let me do with it what I please?' The father granting his request, he travelled away with his money into a distant country, and soon spent it in riotous living.

When he had spent all, there came a time, through all that country, of great public distress and famine, when there was no bread, and the corn, and the grass, and all the things that grow in the ground were all dried up and blighted. The Prodigal Son fell into such distress and hunger, that he hired himself out as a servant to feed swine in the fields. And he would have been glad to eat, even the poor coarse husks that the swine were fed with, but his master gave him none. In this distress, he said to himself "How many of my

---

A FACSIMILE OF A PAGE OF THE MANUSCRIPT OF CHARLES DICKENS'
LIFE OF OUR LORD.

When he had spent all, there came a time, through all that country, of great public distress and famine, when there was no bread, and when the corn, and the grass, and all the things that grow in the ground were all dried up and blighted. The Prodigal Son fell into such distress and hunger, that he hired himself out as a servant to feed swine in the fields. And he would have been glad to eat, even the poor coarse husks that the swine were fed with, but his Master gave him none. In this distress, he said to himself ' How many of my father's servants have bread enough, and to spare, while I perish with hunger ! I will arise and go to my father, and will say unto him, Father ! I have sinned against Heaven, and before thee, and am no more worthy to be called Thy Son ! "

AND so he travelled back again, in
great pain and sorrow and diffi-
culty, to his father's house. When he
was yet a great way off, his father saw
him, and knew him in the midst of all
his rags and misery, and ran towards
him, and wept, and fell upon his neck,
and kissed him. And he told his
servants to clothe this poor repentant
Son in the best robes, and to make
a great feast to celebrate his return.
Which was done ; and they began to
be merry.

But the eldest Son, who had been
in the field and knew nothing of his
brother's return, coming to the house
and hearing the music and Dancing,
called to one of the Servants, and
asked him what it meant. To this
the Servant made answer that his
brother had come home, and that his

72

father was joyful because of his return.
At this, the elder brother was angry
and would not go into the house;
so the father, hearing of it, came out
to persuade him.

'Father', said the elder brother,
'you do not treat me justly, to shew
so much joy for my younger brother's
return. For these many years I have
remained with you constantly, and have
been true to you, yet you have never
made a feast for me. But when my
younger brother returns, who has been
prodigal, and riotous, and spent his
money in many bad ways, you are
full of delight, and the whole house
makes merry!"—"Son," returned the
father, "you have always been with
me, and all I have is yours. But
we thought your brother dead, and
he is alive. He was lost, and he is

found; and it is natural and right that we should be merry for his unexpected return to his old home."

By this, our Saviour meant to teach, that those who have done wrong and forgotten God, are always welcome to him and will always receive his mercy, if they will only return to Him in sorrow for the sin of which they have been guilty.

NOW the Pharisees received these lessons from our Saviour, scornfully; for they were rich, and covetous, and thought themselves superior to all mankind. As a warning to them, Christ related this Parable :—OF DIVES AND LAZARUS.

' There was a certain rich man who was clothed in purple and fine linen, and fared sumptuously every day. And

there was a certain beggar, named
Lazarus, who was laid at his gate,
full of sores, and desiring to be fed
with the crumbs which fell from the
rich man's table. Moreover, the dogs
came and licked his sores.

' And it came to pass that the Beggar
died, and was carried by the angels
into Abraham's bosom—Abraham had
been a very good man who lived many
years before that time, and was then
in Heaven. The rich man also died,
and was buried. And in Hell, he
lifted up his eyes, being in torments,
and saw Abraham afar off, and Lazarus.
And he cried and said, ' Father Abraham
have mercy on me, and send Lazarus
that he may dip the tip of his finger
in water and cool my tongue, for I
am tormented in this flame. But
Abraham said, Son, remember that in

thy life time thou receivedst good
things, and likewise Lazarus evil things.
But now, he is comforted, and thou art
tormented !

A ND among other Parables, Christ
said to these same Pharisees, because of their pride, That two men
once went up into the Temple, to
pray ; of whom, one was a Pharisee,
and one a Publican. The Pharisee
said, ' God I thank Thee, that I am
not unjust as other men are, or bad
as this Publican is ! ' The Publican,
standing afar off, would not lift up
his eyes to Heaven, but struck his
breast, and only said, ' God be merciful
to me, a Sinner ! " And God,—our
Saviour told them—would be merciful
to that man rather than the other,
and would be better pleased with his

prayer, because he made it with a humble and a lowly heart.

The Pharisees were so angry at being taught these things, that they employed some spies to ask Our Saviour questions, and try to entrap Him into saying something which was against the Law. The Emperor of that country, who was called Cæsar, having commanded tribute-money to be regularly paid to him by the people, and being cruel against any one who disputed his right to it, these spies thought they might, perhaps, induce our Saviour to say it was an unjust payment, and so to bring himself under the Emperor's displeasure. Therefore, pretending to be very humble, they came to Him and said, ' Master you teach the word of God rightly, and do not respect persons on account of their wealth

77

or high station. Tell us, is it lawful
that we should pay tribute to Cæsar ? "

Christ, who knew their thoughts,
replied, " Why do you ask ? Shew
me a penny." They did so. " Whose
image, and whose name, is this upon
it ? " he asked them. They said
" Cæsar's." " Then," said He, " Ren-
der unto Cæsar, the things that are
Cæsar's."

So they left him ; very much en-
raged and disappointed that they could
not entrap Him. But our Saviour
knew their hearts and thoughts, as
well as He knew that other men were
conspiring against him, and that he
would soon be put to Death.

As he was teaching them thus, he
sat near the Public Treasury, where
people as they passed along the street,
were accustomed to drop money into

a box for the poor; and many rich persons, passing while Jesus sat there, had put in a great deal of money. At last there came a poor Widow who dropped in two mites, each half a farthing in value, and then went quietly away. Jesus, seeing her do this as he rose to leave the place, called his disciples about him, and said to them that that poor widow had been more truly charitable than all the rest who had given money that day; for the others were rich and would never miss what they had given, but she was very poor, and had given those two mites which might have bought her bread to eat.

Let us never forget what the poor widow did, when we think we are charitable.

CHAPTER THE EIGHTH

THERE was a certain man named Lazarus of Bethany, who was taken very ill; and as he was the Brother of that Mary who had anointed Christ with ointment, and wiped his feet with her hair, She and her sister Martha sent to him in great trouble, saying, Lord, Lazarus whom you love is sick, and like to die.

Jesus did not go to them for two days after receiving this message; but when that time was past, he said to his Disciples, "Lazarus is dead. Let us

80

go to Bethany." When they arrived there (it was a place very near to Jerusalem) they found, as Jesus had foretold, that Lazarus was dead, and had been dead and buried, four days.

When Martha heard that Jesus was coming, she rose up from among the people who had come to condole with her on her poor brother's death, and ran to meet him : leaving her sister Mary weeping, in the house. When Martha saw Him she burst into tears, and said " Oh Lord if Thou hads't been here, my brother would not have died."—" Thy brother shall rise again ", returned Our Saviour. " I know he will, and I believe he will, Lord, at the Resurrection on the Last Day ", said Martha.

Jesus said to her, " I am the Resur-

81

rection and the Life. Dost Thou believe this?" She answered "Yes Lord"; and running back to her sister Mary, told her that Christ was come. Mary hearing this, ran out, followed by all those who had been grieving with her in the house, and coming to the place where he was, fell down at his feet upon the ground and wept; and so did all the rest. Jesus was so full of compassion for their sorrow, that He wept too, as he said, "where have you laid him?"—They said, "Lord, come and see!"

HE was buried in a cave; and there was a great stone laid upon it. When they all came to the Grave, Jesus ordered the stone to be rolled away, which was done. Then, after

82

casting up his eyes, and thanking God, he said, in a loud and solemn voice, " Lazarus, come forth ! " and the dead man, Lazarus, restored to life, came out among the people, and went home with his sisters. At this sight, so awful and affecting, many of the people there, believed that Christ was indeed the Son of God, come to instruct and save mankind. But others ran to tell the Pharisees ; and from that day the Pharisees resolved among themselves —to prevent more people from believing in him, that Jesus should be killed. And they agreed among themselves—meeting in the Temple for that purpose—that if he came into Jerusalem before the Feast of the Passover, which was then approaching, he should be seized.

IT was six days before the Passover, when Jesus raised Lazarus
from the dead ; and, at night, when
they all sat at supper together, with
Lazarus among them, Mary rose up,
and took a pound of ointment (which
was very precious and costly, and was
called ointment of Spikenard) and
anointed the feet of Jesus Christ with
it, and, once again, wiped them on
her hair ; and the whole house was
filled with the pleasant smell of the
ointment. Judas Iscariot, one of the
Disciples, pretended to be angry at
this, and said that the ointment might
have been sold for Three Hundred
Pence, and the money given to the
poor. But he only said so, in reality,
because he carried the Purse, and was
(unknown to the rest, at that time)
a Thief, and wished to get all the

money he could. He now began to plot for betraying Christ into the hands of the chief Priests.

THE Feast of the Passover now drawing very near, Jesus Christ, with his disciples, moved forward towards Jerusalem. When they were come near to that city, He pointed to a village and told two of his disciples to go there, and they would find an ass, with a colt, tied to a tree, which they were to bring to Him. Finding these animals exactly as Jesus had described, they brought them away, and Jesus, riding on the ass, entered Jerusalem. An immense crowd of people collected round him as He went along, and throwing their robes on the ground, and cutting down green branches from the trees, and spreading

85

them in His path, they shouted, and cried " Hosanna to the Son of David ! " (David had been a great King there) " He comes in the name of the Lord ! This is Jesus, the Prophet of Nazareth ! " And when Jesus went into the Temple, and cast out the tables of the money-changers who wrongfully sat there, together with people who sold Doves ; saying " My father's house is a house of prayer, but ye have made it a den of Thieves ! "—and when the people and children cried in the Temple " This is Jesus the Prophet of Nazareth," and would not be silenced—and when the blind and lame came flocking there in crowds, and were healed by his hand—the chief Priests, and Scribes, and Pharisees were filled with fear and hatred of Him. But Jesus continued to heal the sick,

86

and to do good, and went and lodged at Bethany; a place that was very near the City of Jerusalem, but not within the walls.

One night, at that place, he rose from Supper at which he was seated with his Disciples, and taking a cloth and a basin of water, washed their feet. Simon Peter, one of the Disciples, would have prevented Him from washing his feet; but our Saviour told Him that He did this, in order that they, remembering it, might be always kind and gentle to one another, and might know no pride or ill-will among themselves.

Then, he became sad, and grieved, and looking round on the Disciples said, " There is one here, who will betray me." They cried out, one after another, " Is it I, Lord !—" Is it I ! "

But he only answered, " It is one of the Twelve that dippeth with me in the dish." One of the disciples, whom Jesus loved, happening to be leaning on His breast at that moment listening to his words, Simon Peter beckoned to him that he should ask the name of this false man. Jesus answered, " It is he to whom I shall give a sop when I have dipped it in the dish ". and when he had dipped it, He gave it to Judas Iscariot, saying " What thou doest, do quickly." Which the other disciples did not understand, but which Judas knew to mean that Christ had read his bad thoughts.

SO Judas, taking the sop, went out immediately. It was night, and he went straight to the chief Priests and said " what will you give me, if I deliver him to you ? " They agreed to give him thirty pieces of Silver ; and for this, he undertook soon to betray into their hands, his Lord and Master Jesus Christ.

CHAPTER THE NINTH

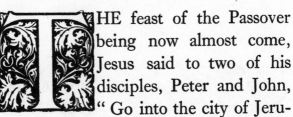HE feast of the Passover being now almost come, Jesus said to two of his disciples, Peter and John, " Go into the city of Jerusalem, and you will meet a man carrying a pitcher of water. Follow him home, and say to him, ' the Master says where is the guest-chamber, where he can eat the Passover with his Disciples.' And he will shew you a large upper room, furnished. There, make ready the supper."

The two disciples found that it happened as Jesus had said ; and having

met the man with the pitcher of water,
and having followed him home, and
having been shewn the room, they
prepared the supper, and Jesus and
the other ten apostles came at the
usual time, and they all sat down to
partake of it together.

It is always called The Last Supper,
because this was the last time that
Our Saviour ate and drank with his
Disciples.

And he took bread from the table,
and blessed it, and broke it, and gave
it to them; and he took the cup
of Wine, and blessed it, and drank,
and gave it to them, saying " Do this
in remembrance of Me ! " And when
they had finished supper, and had sung
a hymn, they went out into the Mount
of Olives.

There, Jesus told them that he would

be seized that night, and that they would all leave him alone and would think only of their own safety. Peter said, earnestly, he never would, for one. " Before the cock crows," returned Our Saviour, " you will deny me thrice." But Peter answered. " No Lord. Though I should die with Thee, I will never deny Thee." And all the other Disciples said the same.

JESUS then led the way over a brook, called Cedron, into a garden that was called Gethsemane ; and walked with three of the disciples into a retired part of the garden. Then he left them as he had left the others, together ; saying " Wait here, and watch ! "—and went away and prayed by Himself, while they, being weary, fell asleep.

92

And Christ suffered great sorrow and distress of mind, in his prayers in that garden, because of the wickedness of the men of Jerusalem who were going to kill Him; and He shed tears before God, and was in deep and strong affliction.

When His prayers were finished, and He was comforted, He returned to the Disciples, and said " Rise! Let us be going! He is close at hand, who will betray me! "

Now, Judas knew that garden well, for Our Saviour had often walked there, with his Disciples; and, almost at the moment when Our Saviour said these words, he came there, accompanied by a strong guard of men and officers, which had been sent by the chief Priests and Pharisees. It being dark, they carried lanterns and torches.

They were armed with swords and staves too; for they did not know but that the people would rise and defend Jesus Christ; and this had made them afraid to seize Him boldly in the day, when he sat teaching the people.

AS the leader of this guard had never seen Jesus Christ and did not know him from the apostles, Judas had said to them, " The man whom I kiss, will be he." As he advanced to give this wicked kiss, Jesus said to the soldiers " Whom do you seek ? " —" Jesus of Nazareth," they answered. " Then," said Our Saviour, " I am He. Let my disciples here, go freely. I am He." Which Judas confirmed, by saying " Hail Master ! " and kissing Him. Whereupon Jesus said,

" Judas, Thou betrayest me with a kiss ! "

The guard then ran forward to seize Him. No one offered to protect Him, except Peter, who, having a sword, drew it, and cut off the right ear of the High Priest's Servant, who was one of them, and whose name was Malchus. But Jesus made him sheath his sword, and gave himself up. Then, all the disciples forsook Him, and fled ; and there remained not one—not one —to bear Him company.

CHAPTER THE TENTH

FTER a short time, Peter and another Disciple took heart, and secretly followed the guard to the house of Caiaphas the High Priest, whither Jesus was taken, and where the Scribes and others were assembled to question Him. Peter stood at the door, but the other disciple, who was known to the High Priest, went in, and presently returning, asked the woman, who kept the door, to admit Peter too. She, looking at him said, " Are you not one of the Disciples ? " He said " I am not." So she let him in; and he stood before a fire that was there, warming himself, among the servants and officers who were crowded round it. For it was very cold.

Some of these men asked him the same question as the woman had done, and said "Are you not one of the disciples?" He again denied it, and said, "I am not." One of them, who was related to that man whose ear Peter had cut off with his sword, said "Did I not see you in the garden with him?" Peter again denied it with an oath, and said "I do not know the man." Immediately the cock crew, and Jesus turning round, looked stedfastly at Peter. Then Peter remembered what He had said—that before the cock crew, he would deny Him thrice—and went out, and wept bitterly.

AMONG other questions that were put to Jesus, the High Priest asked Him what He had taught the people. To which He answered that He had taught them in the open day, and in the open streets, and that the Priests should ask the people what they had learned of Him. One of the officers struck Jesus with his hand for this reply ; and two false witnesses coming in, said they had heard Him say that He could destroy the Temple of God and build it again in three days. Jesus answered little ; but the Scribes and Priests agreed that He was guilty of blasphemy, and should be put to death ; and they spat upon, and beat him.

When Judas Iscariot saw that His Master was indeed condemned, he was so full of horror for what he had done, that he took the Thirty Pieces

98

of Silver back to the chief Priests, and said " I have betrayed innocent blood ! I cannot keep it ! " with those words, he threw the money down upon the floor, and rushing away, wild with despair, hanged himself. The rope, being weak, broke with the weight of his body, and it fell down on the ground, after Death, all bruised and burst,—a dreadful sight to see ! The chief Priests, not knowing what else to do with the Thirty Pieces of Silver, bought a burying-place for strangers with it, the proper name of which was The Potters' Field. But the people called it The Field of Blood ever afterwards.

JESUS was taken from the High Priests' to the Judgment Hall where Pontius Pilate, the Governor, sat, to administer Justice. Pilate (who was not a Jew) said to Him " your own Nation, the Jews, and your own Priests have delivered you to me. What have you done ? " Finding that He had done no harm, Pilate went out and told the Jews so ; but they said " He has been teaching the People what is not true and what is wrong ; and he began to do so, long ago, in Galilee." As Herod had the right to punish people who offended against the law in Galilee, Pilate said, " I find no wrong in him. Let him be taken before Herod ! "

They carried Him accordingly before Herod, where he sat surrounded by his stern soldiers and men in armour. And these laughed at, Jesus, and dressed him, in mockery, in a fine robe, and sent him back to Pilate. And Pilate called the Priests and People together

again, and said " I find no wrong
in this man ; neither does Herod. He
has done nothing to deserve death."
But they cried out, " He has, he has !
Yes, yes ! Let him be killed ! "

Pilate was troubled in his mind to
hear them so clamorous against Jesus
Christ. His wife, too, had dreamed
all night about it, and sent to him
upon the Judgment Seat saying " Have
nothing to do with that just man ! "
As it was the custom at the feast
of the Passover to give some prisoner
his liberty, Pilate endeavoured to persuade the people to ask for the release
of Jesus. But they said (being very
ignorant and passionate, and being told
to do so, by the Priests) " No no,
we will not have him released. Release Barabbas, and let this man be
crucified ! "

Barabbas was a wicked criminal, in jail for his crimes, and in danger of being put to death.

PILATE, finding the people so determined against Jesus, delivered him to the soldiers to be scourged —that is, beaten. They plaited a crown of thorns, and put it on his head, and dressed Him in a purple robe, and spat upon him, and struck him with their hands, and said " Hail, King of the Jews ! "—remembering that the crowd had called him the Son of David when he entered into Jerusalem. And they ill-used him in many cruel ways ; but Jesus bore it patiently, and only said " Father ! Forgive them ! They know not what they do ! "

Once more, Pilate brought Him out before the people, dressed in the purple robe and crown of thorns, and said " Behold the man ! " They cried out, savagely, " Crucify him ! Crucify him ! " So did the chief Priests and officers. " Take him and crucify him yourselves," said Pilate. " I find no fault in him." But they cried out, " He called himself the Son of God ; and that, by the Jewish Law is Death ! And he called himself King of the Jews ; and that is against the Roman Law, for we have no King but Cæsar, who is the Roman Emperor. If you let him go, you are not Cæsar's friend. Crucify him ! Crucify him ! "

When Pilate saw that he could not prevail with them, however hard he tried, he called for water, and washing his hands before the crowd, said, " I am innocent of the blood of this just person." Then he delivered Him to

them to be crucified ; and they, shout-
ing and gathering round Him, and
treating him (who still prayed for them
to God) with cruelty and insult, took
Him away.

CHAPTER THE ELEVENTH

THAT you may know what the People meant when they said " Crucify him ! " I must tell you that in those times, which were very cruel times indeed (let us thank God and Jesus Christ that they are past !) it was the custom to kill people who were sentenced to Death, by nailing them alive on a great wooden Cross, planted upright in the ground, and leaving them there, exposed to the Sun and Wind, and day and night, until they died of pain and thirst. It was the custom too, to make them walk to the place of execution, carrying the cross-piece of wood to which their hands were to be afterwards nailed ; that their shame and suffering might be the greater.

Bearing his Cross, upon his shoulder, like the commonest and most wicked criminal, our blessed Saviour, Jesus Christ, surrounded by the persecuting crowd, went out of Jerusalem to a place called in the Hebrew language, Golgotha ; that is, the place of a scull. And being come to a hill called Mount Calvary, they hammered cruel nails through his hands and feet and nailed him on the Cross, between two other crosses on each of which, a common thief was nailed in agony. Over His head, they fastened this writing " Jesus of Nazareth, the King of the Jews "—

in three languages ; in Hebrew, in Greek, and in Latin.

MEANTIME, a guard of four soldiers, sitting on the ground,
divided His clothes (which they had
taken off) into four parcels for themselves, and cast lots for His coat, and
sat there, gambling and talking, while
He suffered. They offered him vinegar
to drink, mixed with gall ; and wine,
mixed with myrrh ; but he took none.
And the wicked people who passed
that way, mocked him, and said " If
Thou be the Son of God, come down
from the Cross." The Chief Priests
also mocked Him, and said " He came
to save Sinners. Let him save himself ! " One of the thieves too, railed
at him, in his torture, and said, " If
Thou be Christ, save thyself, and

us." But the other Thief, who was penitent, said "Lord! Remember me when Thou comest into Thy Kingdom!" And Jesus answered, "To-day, thou shalt be with me in Paradise."

None were there, to take pity on Him, but one disciple and four women. God blessed those women for their true and tender hearts! They were, the mother of Jesus, his mother's sister, Mary, the wife of Cleophas, and Mary Magdalene who had twice dried his feet upon her hair. The disciple was he whom Jesus loved—John, who had leaned upon his breast and asked Him which was the Betrayer. When Jesus saw them standing at the foot of the Cross, He said to His mother that John would be her son, to comfort her when He was dead; and from that hour John was as a son to her, and loved her.

AT about the sixth hour, a deep and terrible darkness came over all the land, and lasted until the ninth hour, when Jesus cried out, with a loud voice, " My God, My God, why has Thou forsaken me ! " The soldiers, hearing him, dipped a sponge in some vinegar, that was standing there, and fastening it to a long reed, put it up to His Mouth. When He had received it, He said " It is finished ! " —And crying " Father ! Into thy hands I commend my Spirit ! "—died.

Then, there was a dreadful earthquake ; and the Great wall of the Temple, cracked ; and the rocks were rent asunder. The guard, terrified at these sights, said to each other, " Surely this was the Son of God!"—and the People who had been watching the cross from a distance (among whom were many women) smote upon their breasts, and went, fearfully and sadly, home.

The next day, being the Sabbath, the Jews were anxious that the Bodies should be taken down at once, and made that request to Pilate. Therefore some soldiers came, and broke the legs of the two criminals to kill them; but coming to Jesus, and finding Him already dead, they only pierced his side with a spear. From the wound, there came out, blood and water.

There was a good man named Joseph of Arimathea—a Jewish City—who believed in Christ, and going to Pilate privately (for fear of the Jews) begged that he might have the body. Pilate consenting, he and one Nicodemus, rolled it in linen and spices—it was the custom of the Jews to prepare bodies for burial in that way—and buried it in a new tomb or sepulchre, which had been cut out of a rock in a garden near to the place of Crucifixion, and where no one had ever yet been buried. They then rolled a great stone to the mouth of the sepulcher, and left Mary Magdalene, and the other Mary, sitting there, watching it.

THE Chief Priests and Pharisees remembering that Jesus Christ had said to his disciples that He would rise from the grave on the third day after His death, went to Pilate and prayed that the Sepulchre might be well taken care off until that day, lest the disciples should steal the Body, and afterwards say to the people that Christ was risen from the dead. Pilate agreeing to this, a guard of soldiers was set over it constantly, and the stone was sealed up besides. And so it remained, watched and sealed, until the third day; which was the first day of the week.

When that morning began to dawn, Mary Magdalene and the other Mary, and some other women, came to the Sepulchre, with some more spices which they had prepared. As they were saying to each other, " How shall we roll away the stone ? " the earth trembled and shook, and an angel, descending from Heaven, rolled it back, and then sat resting on it. His countenance was like lightning, and his garments were white as snow ; and at sight of

112

him, the men of the guard fainted away with fear, as if they were dead.

MARY MAGDALENE saw the stone rolled away, and waiting to see no more, ran to Peter and John who were coming towards the place, and said " They have taken away the Lord and we know not where they have laid him ! " They immediately ran to the Tomb, but John, being the faster of the two, outran the other, and got there first. He stooped down, and looked in, and saw the linen clothes in which the body had been wrapped, lying there ; but he did not go in. When Peter came up, he went in, and saw the linen clothes lying in one place, and a napkin that had been bound about the head, in another. John also went in, then, and saw the same things. Then they went home, to tell the rest.

But Mary Magdalene remained outside the sepulchre, weeping. After a little time, she stooped down, and looked in, and saw Two angels, clothed in white, sitting where the body of Christ had lain. These said to her, " Woman, why weepest Thou ? " She answered, " Because they have taken away my Lord, and I know not where they have laid him." As she gave this answer, she turned round, and saw Jesus standing behind her, but did not Then know Him. " Woman," said He, " Why weepest Thou ? what seekest thou ? " She, supposing Him to be the gardener, replied, " Sir ! If thou hast borne my Lord hence, tell me where Thou hast laid him, and I will take him away." Jesus pro-

114

nounced her name, "Mary." Then
she knew him, and, starting, exclaimed
" Master ! "—" Touch me not," said
Christ ; " for I am not yet ascended
to my father ; but go to my disciples,
and say unto them, I ascend unto
my Father, and your Father ; and to
my God, and to your God ! "

ACCORDINGLY, Mary Magdalene
went and told the Disciples that
she had seen Christ, and what He
had said to her ; and with them she
found the other women whom she had
left at the Sepulchre when she had
gone to call those two disciples Peter
and John. These women told her and
the rest, that they had seen at the
Tomb, two men in shining garments,
at sight of whom they had been afraid,
and had bent down, but who had

told them that the Lord was risen; and also that as they came to tell this, they had seen Christ, on the way, and had held him by the feet, and worshipped Him. But these accounts seemed to the apostles at that time, as idle tales, and they did not believe them.

The soldiers of the guard too, when they recovered from their fainting-fit, and went to the Chief Priests to tell them what they had seen, were silenced with large sums of money, and were told by them to say that the Disciples had stolen the Body away while they were asleep.

BUT it happened that on that same day, Simon and Cleopas—Simon one of the twelve Apostles, and Cleopas one of the followers of Christ were

116

walking to a village called Emmaus,
at some little distance from Jerusalem,
and were talking, by the way, upon
the death and resurrection of Christ,
when they were joined by a stranger,
who explained the Scriptures to them,
and told them a great deal about God,
so that they wondered at his knowledge. As the night was fast coming
on when they reached the village, they
asked this stranger to stay with them,
which he consented to do. When they
all three sat down to supper, he took
some bread, and blessed it, and broke
it as Christ had done at the Last
Supper. Looking on him in wonder
they found that his face was changed
before them, and that it was Christ
himself ; and as they looked on him,
he disappeared.

They instantly rose up, and returned

to Jerusalem, and finding the disciples sitting together, told them what they had seen. While they were speaking, Jesus suddenly stood in the midst of all the company, and said " Peace be unto ye ! " Seeing that they were greatly frightened, he shewed them his hands and feet, and invited them to touch Him ; and, to encourage them and give them time to recover themselves, he ate a piece of broiled fish and a piece of honeycomb before them all.

BUT Thomas, one of the Twelve Apostles, was not there, at that time ; and when the rest said to him afterwards, " we have seen the Lord ! " he answered " Except I shall see in his hands the print of the nails, and thrust my hand into his side, I will

118

not believe ! " At that moment, though the doors were all shut, Jesus again appeared, standing among them, and said " Peace be unto you ! " Then He said to Thomas, " Reach hither thy finger, and behold my hands ; and reach hither thy hand, and thrust it into my side ; and be not faithless, but believing." And Thomas answered, and said to him, " My Lord and my God ! " Then said Jesus, " Thomas, because thou hast seen me, thou hast believed. Blessed are they that have not seen me, and yet have believed."

AFTER that time, Jesus Christ was seen by five hundred of his followers at once, and He remained with others of them forty days, teaching them, and instructing them to go forth into the world, and preach His gospel and religion ; not minding what wicked men might do to them. And conducting his disciples at last, out of Jerusalem as far as Bethany, he blessed them, and ascended in a cloud to Heaven, and took His place at the right hand of God. And while they gazed into the bright blue sky where He had vanished, two white-robed angels appeared among them, and told them that as they had seen Christ ascend to Heaven, so He would, one day, come descending from it, to judge the World.

WHEN Christ was seen no more, the Apostles began to teach the People as He had commanded them. And having chosen a new apostle, named Matthias, to replace the wicked Judas, they wandered into all countries, telling the People of Christ's Life and Death —and of His Crucifixion and Resurrection—and of the Lessons he had taught—and baptizing them in Christ's name. And through the power He had given them they healed the sick, and gave sight to the Blind, and speech to the Dumb, and Hearing to the Deaf, as he had done. And Peter being thrown into Prison, was delivered from it, in the dead of night, by an Angel : and once, his words before God caused a man named Ananias, and his wife Sapphira, who had told a lie, to be struck down dead, upon the Earth.

Wherever they went, they were persecuted and cruelly treated ; and one man named Saul who had held the clothes of some barbarous persons who pelted one of the Christians named

Stephen, to death with stones, was always active in doing them harm. But God turned Saul's heart afterwards ; for as he was travelling to Damascus to find out some Christians who were there, and drag them to prison, there shone about him a great light from Heaven ; a voice cried, " Saul, Saul, why persecutest thou me ! " and he was struck down from his horse, by an invisible hand, in sight of all the guards and soldiers who were riding with him. When they raised him, they found that he was blind ; and so he remained for three days, neither eating nor drinking, until one of the Christians (sent to him by an angel for that purpose) restored his sight in the name of Jesus Christ. After which, he became a Christian, and preached, and taught,

and believed, with the apostles, and
did great service.

They took the name of Christians
from Our Saviour Christ, and carried
Crosses as their sign, because upon
a Cross He had suffered Death. The
religions that were then in the World
were false and brutal, and encouraged
men to violence. Beasts, and even
men, were killed in the churches, in
the belief that the smell of their blood
was pleasant to the Gods—there were
supposed to be a great many Gods—
and many most cruel and disgusting
ceremonies prevailed. Yet, for all this,
and though the christian Religion was
such a true, and kind, and good one,
the Priests of the old Religions long
persuaded the people to do all possible
hurt to the christians; and christians
were hanged, beheaded, burnt, buried

123

alive, and devoured in Theatres by Wild Beasts for the public amusement, during many years. Nothing would silence them, or terrify them though ; for they knew that if they did their duty, they would go to Heaven. So thousands upon thousands of Christians sprung up and taught the people and were cruelly killed, and were succeeded by other christians, until the Religion gradually became the great religion of the World.

REMEMBER !—It is christianity TO DO GOOD always—even to those who do evil to us. It is christianity to love our neighbour as ourself, and to do to all men as we would have them Do to us. It is christianity to be gentle, merciful, and forgiving, and to keep those qualities quiet in our own hearts, and never make a boast of them, or of our prayers or of our love of God, but always to shew that we love Him by humbly trying to do right in everything. If we do this, and remember the life and lessons of Our Lord Jesus Christ, and try to act up to them, we may confidently hope that God will forgive us our sins and mistakes, and enable us to live and die in Peace.

THE END

drinking, until one of the christians (sent by God an angel for that purpose) restored his sight in the name of Jesus christ. after which, he became a christian, and preached, and taught, and believed; with the apostles, and did great service.

They took the name of christians from Our Saviour christ and carried crosses as their sign, because upon a Cross He had suffered Death. The religions that were then in the world were false and brutal, and encouraged men to violence. Beasts, and even men, were killed in the churches, in the belief, that the smell of their blood was pleasant to the Gods — there were supposed to be a great many Gods — and many most cruel and disgusting ceremonies prevailed. Yet for all this, and though the christian Religion was such a true, and kind, and good one, the Priests of the old Religions long persuaded the people to do all possible hurt to the christians; and christians were beaped, wheeled, burnt, buried alive, and devoured in Theatres by wild Beasts for the public amusement, during many years. Nothing would silence them, or terrify them though; for they knew that if they did their duty they would go to Heaven. So thousands upon thousands of christians sprung up and taught the people and were cruelly killed and were succeeded by other christians, until the Religion gradually became the great religion of the world.

Remember! It is christianity to do Good always — even to those who do Evil to us. It is christianity to love our neighbour as ourself, and to do to all men as we would have them Do to us. It is christianity to be gentle, merciful, and forgiving, and to keep those qualities quiet in our own hearts, and never make a boast of them, or of our prayers, or of our love of God, but always to show that we love Him by humbly trying to do right in everything. If we do this, and remember the life and lessons of Our Lord Jesus christ, and try to act up to them, we may confidently hope that God will forgive us our sins and mistakes, and enable us to live and die in Peace.

A FACSIMILE OF THE LAST PAGE OF THE MANUSCRIPT OF CHARLES DICKENS'
LIFE OF OUR LORD.

APPENDIX

by

Dr. D. JAMES KENNEDY

On page 14, Dickens mistakenly thinks that Jesus was declared God's Son because of His good nature. Rather, the term "the Son of God" is used to describe the second person of the Trinity (John 1:14–18). It is clear from some passages that the term indicated the deity of Jesus Christ (John 5:18–25; Hebrews 1). Therefore, it is incorrect to understand Christ's unique Sonship in an ethical sense.

On page 24, Dickens mistakes the message of Christ as teaching men to become better so they may enter heaven. Rather, Jesus demanded that people commit themselves to Him as their Lord and Savior (John 3:16–18). Jesus claimed that only in union with Him could a person be accepted by God (John 14:6).

On page 28, Dickens confuses being good with the means of getting to heaven. Jesus told the rich young ruler that God alone is good (Matthew 19). Christ called people to confess that they were sinners and to seek forgiveness by coming to Him. Jesus treated forgiveness as a gift that all men needed and that He could bestow.

On page 34, Dickens views the title "Savior" as based upon the character and teaching of Christ. However, the main theological thrust of this term is that Jesus Christ actually is the one who forgives us our sins and grants us eternal life in God's presence. It is Jesus who delivers us from the penalty, power, and presence of sin and therefore is called our Savior.

On page 55, Dickens implies that angels are children. Angels are a separate race of created beings intended to be servants of God and His people (Hebrews 1 and 2). They are not children, nor are they any other type of human being. However, it is true that one of the duties of angels is to watch over small children (Matt. 18:10).

On pages 58 and 59, Dickens correctly points out that repentant sinners can be forgiven by God because of Christ. However, he fails to see that there are none who are so good that they do not need repentance. The Bible would teach that all are sinners and in need of salvation.

Romans chapter 4 clearly teaches that Abraham was accepted by God because he believed in God's redemptive promises. Dickens, on pages 75 and 76, implies that Abraham was saved because of his good works.

On page 124, Dickens implies that heaven is earned by doing one's duty. However, when asked what work a person could do to have eternal life, Jesus said, "This is the work of God, that ye believe on him whom he hath sent" (John 6:29, KJV). Dickens' concern for good deeds and duty are admirable, but these good works are the results of having come into a proper relationship with God, not a means to achieve eternal life.

The high edicts Dickens recommends to his children are desperately needed by the youth of our age. However, on page 125 he fails to recognize that those who truly believe in Jesus Christ as Lord and Savior, and manifest this in their lives through good deeds, can *know* that they have eternal life (1 John 5:13). God first forgives and cleanses us, and then creates in us the ability and desire to serve Him (Eph. 2:8–10).

128